The World's Wildest Places

Written by
Lily Dyu

Illustrated by
Riley Samels

Contents

Venezuela 8-11

is on the northern coast of South America with many islands in the Caribbean Sea. It is home to Angel Falls – the world's highest uninterrupted waterfall – at almost 1,000 metres (1,280 ft) tall.

Malaysian Borneo 12-15

Borneo is the third largest island in the world, with a population of 6.8 million people – about the same as London. Straddling the equator, the island is shared between three countries. Malaysian Borneo covers around one quarter of the island.

Mexico 16-19

is a large country with a rich mixture of European and Indigenous cultures. Its location between the Arctic Circle to the north and the equator to the south makes it a refuge for animals fleeing extreme cold or heat.

Armenia 20-23

is a small country, similar in size to the US state of South Carolina. It lies in the Caucasus – a region between the Caspian Sea and the Black Sea that spans both Europe and Asia. The Caucasus includes parts of Georgia, Armenia, Azerbaijan, Russia, Iran, and Turkey.

Kenya 24-27

straddles the equator and borders the Indian Ocean. The dramatic Great Rift Valley runs through the middle of the country. The valley wasn't formed by river erosion, but is a result of the earth's crust slowly pulling apart.

Peru 28-31

is on the western side of South America. It is home to both part of the Amazon Rainforest and the ancient city of Machu Picchu.

The Philippines 32-35

is is made up of more than 7,640 islands rather than one big land mass. This is called an archipelagic country.

Vietnam 36-39

is a long, narrow "S"-shaped country in Southeast Asia. It is roughly half the size of France. At its narrowest point, the country is just over 30 miles (48 km) wide!

UK 40-43

is an island country in the Atlantic Ocean that lies off the north-west coast of mainland Europe. It is made up of four parts: England, Scotland, Wales, and Northern Ireland.

Belize 44-47

is a tiny country about the size of Wales. It has a long coastline and the world's second largest coral reef after Australia's Great Barrier Reef. Mayan civilizations existed in Belize for almost 3,000 years.

Zambia 48-51

is a land-locked country in Africa, set mostly on a high plateau which makes it look much flatter than its mountainous neighbours. Its name comes from the Zambezi River that runs through it.

Mexico

Belize

Guatemala

Venezuela

Colombia

Ecuador

Peru

Brazil

Bolivia

Paraguay

Argentina

Which wild place

UK

Armenia

Cameroon

Vietnam

India

Philippines

Borneo

Kenya

Zambia

will you visit today?

Foreword

Imagine some of the oldest forests in the world, where orangutans roam alongside elephants, pangolins, hornbills, and leopards. Imagine you had the power to save these forests – which are home to hundreds of species – simply by reading a book.

Stop imagining! That is exactly what you've done by picking up this copy of *The World's Wildest Places*. This is a book that will support the work of a charity I'm a patron of – World Land Trust (WLT). From the moment you first flipped open the cover, you unleashed the magic of conservation onto the world. Proceeds from every copy – including the one you're holding – will help WLT to fund the saving of spectacular wild places.

One of the landscapes you'll be helping to protect is the rainforest along the Kinabatangan River in Malaysian Borneo. This is a place I first visited in 1991, and I've returned every five years or so since. I've seen how quickly and dramatically it's changed, becoming easily the most precious and beleaguered primary rainforest on earth. Thanks to WLT – and thanks to you – it's being given another chance.

What WLT do is very simple – they help to save wild places before others can destroy them. They help to save land, and then put it into the hands of local communities. People like Berjaya Elahan, the ranger who patrols Borneo's rainforests day and night to keep wildlife safe. It's simple and yet it gives back something huge: orangutans can live in peace, while people like you and I get to live on a planet where the carbon stored in rainforest trees is kept away from the atmosphere. All of us safer – forever.

The easiest way to understand the might of wild places is to be in them. The next time you visit a forest, look around you. Look up at the canopy of trees that clean the air you breathe and help us all fight climate change by absorbing carbon. Look down at the mushroom stalks, and the green moss twisting along tree roots; look out for the birds that call as you walk along the forest floor, and the deer that leap away when you get too close. Everything connected, everything alive, because the forest was left standing. That is the power of wild places – that is what they do for us all when we protect them.

Today, as you go on to discover all the natural wonders that await in the pages of this book – from Borneo's orangutan valleys to Armenia's Caucasian leopard refuge, Brazil's Atlantic Forest, and Zambia's elephant heartlands – I want you to remember something: by getting this book and supporting the conservation work of WLT, you've already done so much to save amazing landscapes like these. All that's left is for you to read about them and tell your friends and family about them, too. Together, we can make sure everyone learns about the power of wild places, but also our own power to save them.

This is what I want you to never forget as you set off on this new journey to discover wild places – no one is ever too small to make a difference for the planet.

Who are WLT?

Founded in 1989, World Land Trust (WLT) is a charity that seeks to protect the world's most biologically significant and threatened habitats. Through a network of partner organizations around the world, WLT funds the creation of reserves that are then protected permanently for habitats and wildlife.

Since being founded, donations to WLT have allowed their partners to bring almost 2.5 million acres into protection – an area the size of the island of Jamaica. These protected acres have, in turn, allowed WLT partners to connect more than 25 million acres of precious habitats – an area the size of Iceland – linked by corridors for wildlife to travel through safety. And that's not all! Over the years, WLT supporters have funded the planting of an astounding 2,457,900 native trees around the world.

By protecting habitats and then restoring them through tree planting, WLT supporters have made a difference for a spectacular array of species. Almost 10,000 species are known to live in WLT partner project areas around the world. Of that, 3,871 are bird species, followed by plants (3,036), mammals (856), insects and other invertebrates (676), reptiles (634), fish (362), and amphibian (348) species.

Throughout this book, you'll be finding out about some of the amazing animals that WLT partners protect every day: Argentina's pumas, Borneo's orangutans, Brazil's toucans, Colombia's manatees, Ecuador's sloths, India's tigers, Kenya's elephants, Peru's bears, Zambia's zebras – and too many others to list here. *The World's Wildest Places* will not just introduce you to these incredible species. It will also open a window into the majestic landscapes they call home. From Armenia's snow-capped peaks to Mexico's misty cloud forests and Paraguay's dusty Dry Chaco vastness, no two habitats you read about are the same, but all have one thing in common: they are being protected by WLT partners and everyone – wildlife, but also people – is benefitting.

As WLT Patron Steve Backshall mentioned, proceeds from this book will support the work of WLT's conservation partners, like Guyra Paraguay ranger Lourdes Matoso – you can see her on the left in the picture below – or the Cameroonians who are protecting the gorilla habitat they know best. And that's what we hope you will remember as you go on to discover these wonderful wild places – that the people who are keeping them safe are not doing it alone. You, the person who is holding this book, stand alongside them.

From WLT and its partners, thank you for believing in a world of wild places!

Venezuela

On Venezuela's Margarita Island, an iguana is clambering up a cactus on a mission to find food. There's a streak of pink in the sky as a flock of flamingos pass by on their way to feeding grounds on the coast. On reaching the top of the cactus, the iguana spies some tasty, red flowers on a nearby plant. He leaps from his prickly perch across to its neighbour, which wobbles precariously as he lands. Soon, he's feasting on juicy, young buds, not minding their spiny coats. When his meal is finished, the iguana starts searching for a comfortable spot on the ground. It's the hottest part of the day, and the perfect time to go and bask in the sun...

What can you see?

Bullet ant

Blue-crowned parakeet

Venezuelan poodle moth

The habitat

Venezuela has a variety of habitats, from Caribbean coastline to the peaks of the Andes. Margarita Island is off the north coast of the mainland. It is a mixture of thorny shrubland, cacti, and dry forests.

The Chacaracual Reserve was created to protect wildlife like the ocelot, the Margarita white-tailed deer, the southern long-nosed bat, and the endangered yellow-shouldered parrots that are unique to the island.

Trees
Trees and shrubs don't grow very high

Land
The land here is typically flat

Green iguana
They can detach their tails if they are caught by a predator. This doesn't cause them any damage – they just grow a new one!

Melon cactus
This plant is sometimes called the Turk's cap because of the red cap on the top, which looks like a Fez hat.

Thorny shrubland

This habitat is often found at the base of a mountain range. It has a temperate climate. This means that the temperature is not extreme at any time of the year.

Yellow-shouldered parrot
This bird is very social and can often be found in groups of up to 700 birds.

Prickly pear cactus
Humans can eat the pads of the prickly pear cactus – as long as the thorns are removed first!

Margarita white-tailed deer
This subspecies of white-tailed deer is endemic to Venezuela. It wags its tail when it senses danger.

Did you spot them all?

Bullet ant
Bullet ants are the biggest ants in the world! Their sting is thirty times more painful than a bee's, and it takes twenty four hours for the pain of the sting to wear off completely.

Santa Cruz water lily

This lily can grow up to 2 metres (6½ ft) wide and can support the weight of a small child!

The people helping

Pablo Millán camps out in the Chacaracual Community Reserve twenty four hours a day during breeding season. He protects the nests of yellow-shouldered parrots from poachers. He also checks on their newly hatched eggs and helps to guard them from natural predators, like snakes and hawks.

Illegal hunting and illegal trafficking of animals and plants are great threats to wildlife survival. Without protection, yellow-shouldered parrots are often stolen from their nests and sold as pets.

Southern long-nosed bat

They can live to be 30 years old in the wild.

American flamingo

Their feather colour comes from the food they eat.

Crab-eating fox

It can dig its own den, but prefers to live in burrows that have been dug by other animals.

How you can help

Our world is changing, and not all birds are able to change along with it. You can help by making your garden bird-friendly and putting out food and water for our feathered friends.

Blue-crowned parakeet

There are fewer than 100 of these birds on Margarita Island in Venezuela. They can travel long distances between their roosts and feeding areas, but they can also adapt their diet to the food that is available.

Venezuelan poodle moth

The Venezuelan poodle moth was only discovered in 2009, so scientists still don't know very much about it. They believe it is only around 2½ cm (1 inch) in length.

Malaysian Borneo

It's dawn on the Kinabatangan River in Malaysian Borneo. Visitors have risen early to see the rainforest wake and to catch a glimpse of the amazing wildlife. The skipper cuts the boat's engine and lets it drift. Mist hugs the river as sunrise starts to bleach the darkness. It's warm and sticky, and the air carries the scent of the jungle – earth, vegetation, and decaying wood. Ferns, orchids, and moss cover the tree trunks. Above, the canopy is full of life. A colourful hornbill perches next to its nest, while a monkey crashes through the branches. The noise of birdsong and insects is almost deafening.

What can you see?

Pyrops intricatus

Wreathed hornbill

Orchid mantis

The habitat

Borneo's rainforest is estimated to be 130 million years old – the oldest in the world. The Kinabatangan is Malaysia's second longest river. It is often called the "Amazon of the East."

The Keruak Corridor is a wildlife corridor that protects many species, such as the pygmy elephant, the proboscis monkey, and orangutans. It's one of only two places in the world where you can see orangutans in the wild – the other is Indonesia.

Bornean elephant

It is smaller and friendlier than the Asian elephant. They are good swimmers that can easily cross rivers.

Pitcher plant

These plants are carnivorous – this means that they feast on other living creatures!

Plants

There are fewer different types of plants in these forests

River

Swamp forests are most often found on the lower parts of rivers

Freshwater swamp forest

These forests are flooded with freshwater either permanently or seasonally.

Sun bear

Their name comes from the light patch of fur on their chest. Legend has it that the patch represents the rising sun.

Sunda clouded leopard

Their name comes from the cloud-like markings on their fur.

Did you spot them all?

Pyrops intricatus

The pyrops intricatus is from a family of bugs that has the nickname "lanternflies." It was believed that their snouts glowed at night, but this has since been found not to be true. Nevertheless, the nickname has stuck.

Oriental dwarf kingfisher

They build horizontal nests that can be up to one metre (3 ft) in length.

The people helping

Daisah Bin Kapar follows orangutans around the rainforest. She is working to connect fragments of rainforest by creating wildlife corridors that animals can safely use. This will give them more space to roam, hunt, and mate.

The floodplain around the Kinabatangan River has already lost 80% of its forest to palm oil plantations. What was once one big forest is now smaller, fragmented parts.

Corpse flower

They are the world's largest flower. But don't sniff too deeply, as they smell of rotting fish!

Orangutan

They eat, sleep, and travel in the canopies of tropical rainforests. They are the world's largest tree-dwelling mammal.

Proboscis monkey

The male proboscis monkey's big nose helps them make loud mating calls.

How you can help

Palm oil is everywhere, from pizza to chocolate, shampoo to lipstick. Look for products that use responsibly sourced palm oil. This means that the farmer has grown the palm oil without harming people, wildlife, or the environment.

Wreathed hornbill

The throat of a young wreathed hornbill is blue. As they get older, the male hornbill's throat will turn bright yellow, but the female's will stay blue. This is an easy way to tell the sexes apart.

Orchid mantis

The orchid mantis may look like a flower and have a name like a flower, but it's really an insect. Its appearance helps it to attract bees and other insects, which it can then feast on.

Mexico

In the Sierra Gorda mountains of Central Mexico, Monarch butterflies stir from their sleep as the morning sun begins to warm the forest. They blanket the oaks and pines so thickly that branches sag under their weight. What at first looks like blossom bursts from the trees as the creatures wake and stretch their wings. Soon the air gently thrums as thousands of butterflies take flight. The delicate insects rise like a glowing cloud in the blue sky to continue their journey south. Starting from Canada and America, they have been travelling for almost two months. But now they're nearly at their destination – their wintering grounds in southwest Mexico. They'll shelter there until the spring, in the very same trees their ancestors used before them.

What can you see?

Bell's false brook salamander

Butterwort

Bearded wood-partridge

The habitat

Most of Mexico's land is a plateau – a raised flat area – surrounded by mountains. The area also has dry, semi-desert carpeted in cacti and yukka as well as misty, magical cloud forests.

Lying in Mexico's highlands, the Sierra Gorda Biosphere Reserve is a treasure trove of the wild. Its forests are home to the powerful puma as well as threatened birds like the multi-coloured military macaw.

Puma

It can adapt to different environments, from deserts to mountains. Adults are usually all one colour, but their cubs are born with spotted coats.

Soil

Plants don't grow here easily as the soil is sandy

Southern flying squirrel

They cannot fly like a bird, but they can glide. They use their legs to steer and their tail to brake!

Plant life

The plants that can grow here often have glossy leaves that reflect the sunlight

Semi-arid desert

These deserts are cooler than arid deserts like the Sahara. Long, dry summers are followed by some rainfall in the winter.

Bumblebee hummingbird

They are the second smallest known bird and are about the same size as a bumblebee!

Magnolia tree

They are one of the most ancient species of plants.

Military macaw

These noisy birds have a creaky sounding call, but they quickly fall silent when predators are nearby.

Did you spot them all?

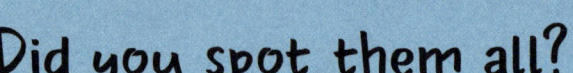

Bell's false brook salamander

These salamanders are only found in Mexico. They don't have lungs and instead "breathe" through their skin. They must keep themselves moist to absorb oxygen.

Emerald toucanet

They live in the forest canopy. Their bright colours actually help to camouflage them among the leaves.

Monarch butterfly

A Monarch butterfly travels as far as 100 miles (160 km) a day during its annual 3,000-mile migration south. During its journey, it relies on the huge amount of food it ate when it was a caterpillar for fuel.

Wildlife habitat is threatened by illegal logging. Large, mature trees are chopped down for just a small piece of wood, and the logger sells this for a small sum. These trees then take a long time to grow again.

Flowering cactus

They grow on limestone rocks, high above sea level.

Black bear

It marks its territory by leaving scratches and bite marks on trees.

The people helping

Pati Ruiz and her son Roberto work to protect the Sierra Gorda Biosphere Reserve. They encourage landowners to switch to nature-friendly farming and help them to receive funding for protecting their forests. They have also supported women to get jobs in eco-tourism.

How you can help

Butterflies frequently visit gardens in autumn to feed and build up reserves for the winter. Leave fallen fruit on the ground for them, or put out some of your own - mushy bananas and soft mangoes are their favourites.

Butterwort

Its sticky leaves catch small bugs. If temperatures drop or there is a drought, a butterwort sheds their sticky leaves and grows succulent foliage. So it is like two plants in one!

Bearded wood-partridge

These birds are endemic to Mexico and at risk of extinction. They are shy and will run away quickly rather than fly if they come into contact with humans.

Armenia

It's late afternoon, and on a hillside in Armenia's Caucasus region, a herdsman calls to his cattle. It's time to get them back to the village, safely away from the wolves and bears that roam here. It's May, and the pastures are a riot of colour and carpeted in wildflowers as far as the eye can see. Purple irises, blue cornflowers, and red poppies breathe their sweet scent into the warm breeze. Butterflies and insects form trembling clouds above the swaying blooms. A bearded vulture soars majestically overhead. Its huge wings are like a black comb in the blue sky. In the distance, the highest mountains are still cloaked with snow.

What can
you see?

Tomares romanov
butterfly

Least weasel

Purple iris

21

The habitat

More than 80% of the land in Armenia is mountainous. Although it is rugged, the Caucasus region is home to hundreds of species of mammals and birds.

The Caucasus Wildlife Refuge protects amazing creatures like the lynx and the bezoar goat. There are also many types of birds here, including four species of vulture.

Bearded vulture

The feathers of adults are actually mostly white, but they are dyed orange by the water the birds bathe in.

Bezoar goat

The horns of the male bezoar goat make them instantly recognizable. They curve upwards and backwards in an arc shape and are highly prized by hunters.

Caucasian leopard

They growl and roar, but they also purr when they are happy! Their spot patterns are unique – like snowflakes – and can be used to identify them.

Grassland

Grasslands help in the fight against global warming, as they are able to absorb carbon dioxide

Alpine steppe

This habitat is a mixture of woodland and grasslands. They have long, cold winters and short summers, but it doesn't rain much at all.

Brown bear

The largest predator still living on the continent of Europe is the brown bear. Despite their weight, the animals can run at speeds of up to 30 miles (50 km) per hour!

Did you spot them all?

Tomares romanov butterfly

Like other butterflies, the tomares romanov butterfly chooses a host plant. The female will lay her eggs on the leaves, and when the larvae hatch, they will begin to eat the plant.

Armenian viper

They live on dry, rocky slopes at high elevations. Their tongues help them to sniff out food, predators, and mates.

The people helping

Boris Vanyan is one of the rangers who patrols the Caucasus Wildlife Refuge. One of his main jobs is to keep the trail cameras working. These cameras track leopards, record their movements, and help keep them safe from hunters.

Grey wolf

Their howl can be heard up to 10 miles (16 km) away, and they howl more during a full moon.

Pinkish poppy

The endangered pinkish poppy is endemic to Armenia.

Illegal hunting and poaching are a huge threat to wildlife, because rare species can be sold for a high price.

Mountain alcon blue butterfly

When mountain alcon blue butterflies are larvae, they trick ants into thinking that they are ant larvae. The ants then bring food back to the butterfly larvae for them to eat.

European roller

Their name comes from the acrobatic moves they perform while in the air.

How you can help

Wildflowers provide nectar for pollinators such as bees and butterflies. These pollinators then help provide food for both wildlife and people. You can help our pollinators by planting wildflower seeds. All you need is a pot or a patch of ground.

Least weasel

Least weasels are very adaptable creatures and can live in lots of different habitats, from grasslands to rainforests. They are also able to live both above and below ground.

Purple iris

Armenia is home to lots of species of Iris plants. However, many of them are toxic, and just touching them can cause an allergic reaction!

Kenya

Day breaks over the Kenyan savannah. A family of giraffe munch on leaves from the high branches of an acacia tree, while zebra graze in the scorched grass around them. A rhinoceros and her calf wallow at the edge of a lake. They know the cooling mud will protect them from the midday sun and bugs. In the distance, the morning sun slowly spreads across the jagged, crown-like outline of Mount Kenya. Soon, the whole mountain is glowing ~ from its snow-capped peak to its lower slopes. Here, a patchwork of leafy, green forests are home to a myriad of wildlife, including monkeys and elephants. In the treetops, birds of every shape, size, and colour raucously welcome in the new day.

What can you see?

Lowland bongo

Sharpe's longclaw

Crowned hawk eagle

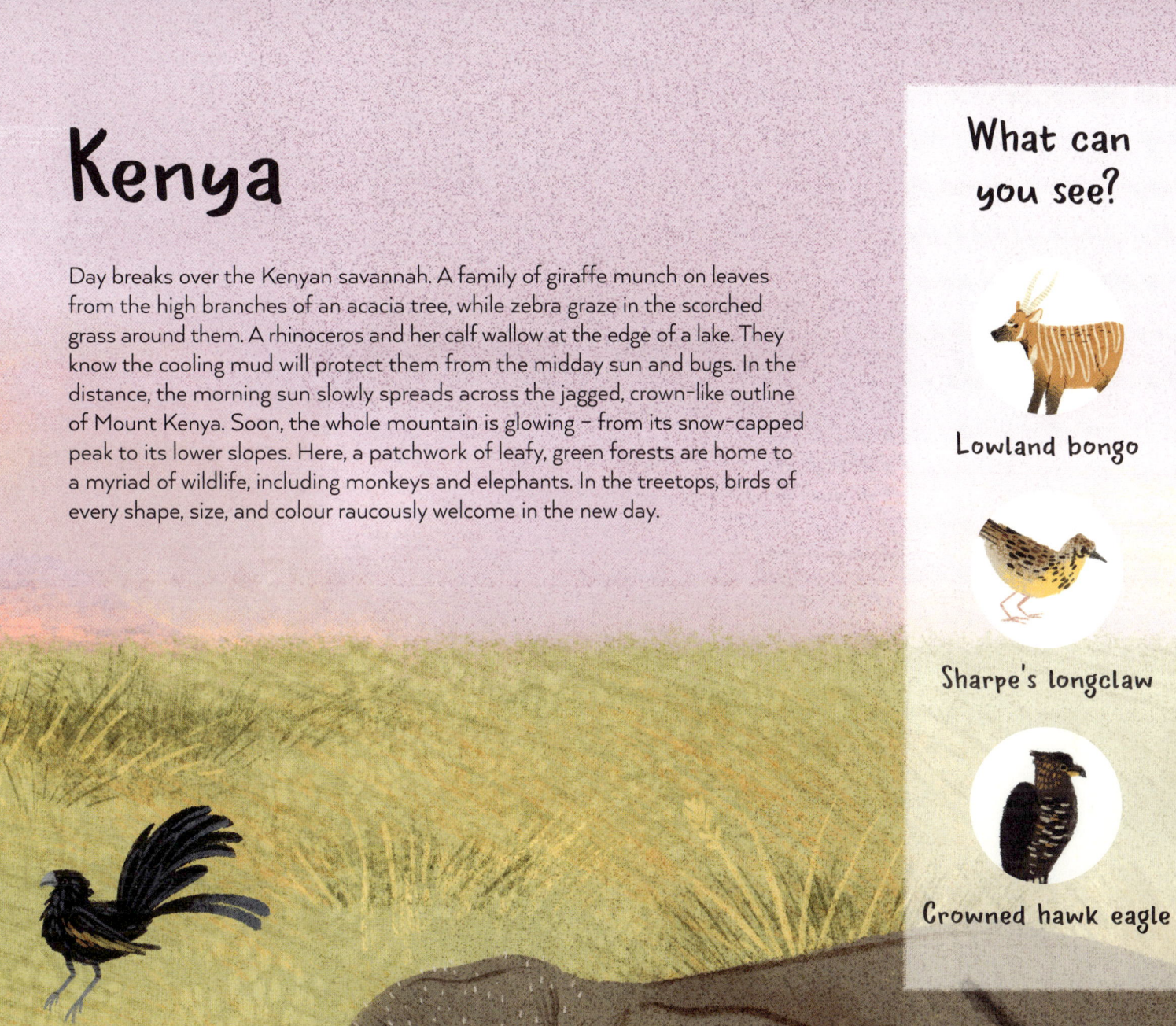

The habitat

Kenya is best known for its savannah where you might see Africa's "Big Five" – lions, leopards, elephants, buffalo, and rhinos. But the country has a great variety of landscapes and habitats – from tropical rainforests and coast, to moorland and mountains.

In the Mount Kenya Forest Reserve and the Kikuyu Escarpment forest, fast growing native trees are being planted. These will help to provide food and shelter for the huge diversity of life here.

Giraffe

A giraffe's neck is too short to reach the ground. They have to kneel to drink water.

Mountain

Mount Kenya is between two and five million years old

Parasol tree

It is also known as the umbrella tree because of its shape.

Plant life

The flora of montane moorlands is not very diverse

Montane moorland

The climate at this high altitude is extreme and changes very quickly. Days feel like summer, but nights feel like winter.

Red chested owlet

They are active and vocal during the day, which can cause angry songbirds to mob them!

Plains zebra

They have excellent vision and hearing. This means that they can detect an approaching predator early.

Did you spot them all?

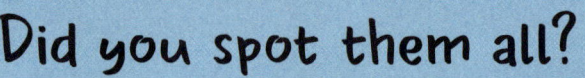

Lowland bongo

These antelopes have herbivorous diets. This means that they only eat plants, but they also visit natural mineral licks to get the salts they need to stay healthy.

Leopard orchids

They are named for the pattern on their leaves. They grow on the higher branches of taller trees, because they need light to bloom.

Black rhino

They are actually grey, but their skin colour can vary, because they like to wallow in mud and dust. They do most of their foraging at night.

Water hyacinth

They are a big problem on Kenya's Lake Victoria, where they stop fishing boats getting around. But scientists are exploring whether they can be turned into biofuel for people to cook with.

The greatest threat to wildlife is deforestation because of Kenya's growing population. Trees are being cut down to provide farmland, and grasslands are being converted for crops. Fragmented habitats disrupt the movement of wildlife.

Elephant shrew

They use their tails to mark their territory.

Jackson's widowbird

Male Jackson's widowbirds jump straight up into the air as part of their mating ritual.

The people helping

Local people are collecting seeds, growing native seedlings, and replanting trees on the reserve. Many are also switching to more nature-friendly jobs, such as beekeeping, spinning wool, and farming butterflies.

How you can help

You can help reduce the number of trees being chopped down. Save paper by using both sides of the same piece, don't print things out if you don't need to, and recycle paper and cardboard.

Sharpe's longclaw

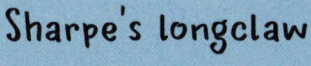

They depend on tussock grasses for survival. Tussock grasses grow in clumps in dry habitats. Sharpe's longclaws nest, feed, and hide from predators in these grasses.

Crowned hawk eagle

They aren't the world's biggest eagle, but they are the world's most powerful eagle. They are able to kill prey that is up to four times bigger than they are using a long talon on their back toes.

Peru

High in a cloud forest in northern Peru, waterfalls tumble down a rocky
mountainside, while patches of mist drift around the canopy of the trees.
Here, a dark brown bear is climbing a wild avocado tree. The tree's trunk
is thick with moss and orchids, and straggly air plants hang from nooks
in the boughs. Water drips down to the forest floor, where hummingbirds
hover between blooms. On reaching the top of the avocado tree, the bear
pulls down a clump of green fruit and tastes one. They're almost, but not
quite, ripe. She lets the fruit fall before settling back comfortably into the
curve of a thick branch. She is happy to wait until the feast is ready to eat.

What can
you see?

Marvellous
spatuletail

Andean night
monkey

Peruvian coral snake

The habitat

Peru has dramatic landscapes, from deserts and paramo, to the Andes mountains and the Amazon rainforest. Peru's cloud forests are amazingly biodiverse.

The Tabaconas Nambelle-Yacuri Corridor is helping to protect the cloud forests and the animals that live there. These include the vulnerable spectacled bear, various incredible reptiles and amphibians, and birds such as the red-faced parrot and golden-plumed parakeet.

Clouds

They are present all year round

Red howler monkey

They like to sit in the canopies of trees for long periods of time, munching on leaves.

Plants

The high humidity helps air plants, moss, and ferns to grow.

Red-faced parrot

They make different calls when they are flying and when they are perched.

Cloud forest

Cloud forests are found where higher altitude rainforests meet the mountains, and warm, moist air is pushed upwards to form condensation.

Dragon blood tree

If you cut the bark of the dragon blood tree, it seeps a dark red, foamy sap. Local people use this as medicine.

Andean condor

This is the largest flying bird in the world. It has a wingspan of more than three metres (9½ ft)!

Did you spot them all?

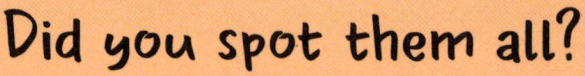

Marvellous spatuletail

This spectacular hummingbird is unique among birds for having just four feathers in its tail. It can move one of its outer tail feathers without moving the other.

Amazon lily

The sweet-scented Amazon lily has star-shaped clusters of white flowers in groups of four. It is dormant at near freezing temperatures.

Lots of metals are mined in Peru. Forests are chopped down to make way for the mines, and mining activities then pollute surrounding rivers and streams.

The people helping

Many local communities own their land, and they are creating community wildlife reserves. These connect to form important wildlife corridors, and they also protect the area from mining. Local people are also learning new, nature-friendly ways to farm sustainably.

Neblina metaltail

These hummingbirds live in the same habitat all year round – even in extreme weather.

Mountain tapir

It can use its nose to grab fruit, leaves, and other food that is out of its reach.

Spectacled bear

They were the inspiration for Paddington Bear. The storybook bear loves marmalade, but the real-life bears prefer honey.

How you can help

Humans are using up Earth's resources through mining, overconsumption, and throwing things into landfill. You can help by recycling and buying fewer new things. Hidden inside old electronic items and batteries are metals and minerals that can be reused.

Andean night monkey

These nocturnal monkeys spend the daytime sleeping in tree hollows, among vines, or in piles of leaves and sticks. A common monkey pastime is to groom each other, but Andean night monkeys haven't been seen doing this.

Peruvian coral snake

The fangs of this venomous snake are hollow and quite short, but they're always ready to bite. They hold onto their prey when they attack, waiting for the venom to take effect.

The Philippines

A green turtle paddles slowly through the warm, turquoise water of the Sulu Sea. Beneath her, endless meadows of coral throng with colour and life. Yellow and black angel fish glide through anemone forests while a lobster scuttles between rocks. Shoals of silvery fish shimmer in shafts of sunlight as a giant electric-blue clam slowly opens its shell to feast on plankton. The water becomes shallower as the turtle approaches her destination of Danjugan Island. Soon she will reach its pristine white shores, but first, she drops onto the seabed to feed on seagrass. It's her last chance to eat before clambering up the beach to lay and bury her eggs.

What can you see?

Blue-ringed octopus

Giant clam

Bargibant's pygmy seahorse

The habitat

Danjugan is a tiny island rising from the Sulu Sea. It is one of the Philippines' thousands of islands. Its main habitats are tropical rainforests, mangroves, and coral reefs.

Danjugan Island was once threatened with development. Today it is a marine reserve and wildlife sanctuary protecting species including turtles, dolphins, sharks, birds, butterflies, and bats.

Seagrass

Seagrass meadows help to protect the shore against waves and storm

White-breasted sea eagle

The call of the white-breasted sea eagle is a loud honking – like a goose.

Hard coral

These are the species that build the reefs

Blacktip reef shark

Female blacktip reef sharks can reproduce without a male mate.

Tiger tail seahorse

Like all seahorses, tiger tail seahorses are slow swimmers. However, they are able to move backwards as well as forwards and up and down.

Fringing coral reef

Coral reefs are underwater structures made up of different shaped and sized coral. Fringing coral reefs are the most common type of coral reef. They grow near the coastlines of islands but are separated from the shoreline by lagoons.

Green sea turtle

They can live for up to 80 years. The females travel thousands of miles to return to the beaches where they were born to lay their eggs.

Coral

People often think coral are plants, but they're wrong. Coral are actually animals that have attached themselves to the ocean floor.

Did you spot them all?

Blue-ringed octopus

The tiny blue-ringed octopus is one of the most dangerous animals in the ocean. Each one contains enough venom to kill 26 people, but its bite is painless.

Golden-crowned flying fox

It is one of the world's largest bats. It has a wingspan of 1½ metres (5 ft) – that's longer than most children! It can only be found in the Philippines.

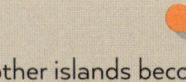

Clownfish

All clownfish are born male, but they are able to become female.

As other islands become developed, Danjugan Island is even more important for endemic and migrating wildlife. But global warming is causing rising sea levels which are eroding the island's shores.

Sea anemones

They use their tentacles to catch food as it floats by.

The people helping

When students visit Danjugan Island, Chai Apale is in charge of teaching them about the animals that live there and how important conservation is. She is a marine biologist, and so she loves to scuba dive to check on the coral.

Tarsier

They can turn their head 180 degrees to look around. This is handy, because their eyes are fixed in place.

Dugong

These herbivores do not need complicated schemes to catch their food.

How you can help

Plastic rubbish can kill sea creatures who may eat it or become tangled in it. You can help by joining a beach clean, picking up litter, and avoiding single-use plastics, like plastic bags, straws, and food wrappers.

Giant clam

They typically weigh around 200 kg (440 lb) and can live for up to 100 years! Legend has it that giant clams can swallow a human whole, but this isn't true. The clam's shell closes too slowly for this to happen.

Bargibant's pygmy seahorse

These seahorses are the same colour as the coral they live on. They are usually either purple and pink or yellow and orange.

What can you see?

Owston's civit

Edward's pheasant

Crested argus

Vietnam

It's early morning in Vietnam's Khe Nuoc Trong reserve. Dense green forest blankets the land, and jagged emerald hills stretch as far as the eye can see. Mist rises from the valleys, hiding the rivers that snake beneath. The faces of red-shanked douc peer out from the treetops, and the air is already alive with birdsong, the croaking of frogs, and the whir of cicadas. Suddenly, the haunting call of a female gibbon echoes around the mountainsides. Her mate joins in, eventually followed by their young. Further down the valley, another gibbon family answers. Soon the forest is a cacophony of sound from every direction.

The habitat

Forest, savannah, brushland, and bamboo cover half of Vietnam's land area. There are more than 1,500 species of trees here – that's more than the whole of America. Khe Nuoc Trong reserve protects trees in the evergreen forests in the country's centre.

Khe Nuoc Trong forest is rich in birdlife – including the crested argus – plus rare reptiles and amphibians. Endangered species, including the red-shanked douc langur and southern white-cheeked gibbon, can also be found here.

Hopea tree

It has small, sweet-scented, yellow-white flowers and bears fruit. It produces a resin that can be used to heal wounds.

Trees

The canopies in these forests have three tiers.

Evergreen forest

More than 80% of the trees in an evergreen forest do not completely shed their leaves seasonally.

Bamboo

This is the world's fastest growing plant.

Reticulated python

They are the longest snakes in the world. They aren't venomous, and they are not usually dangerous to humans, although there are records of them eating people!

Sunda pangolin

They do not have teeth. Instead, their food is ground up by their stomach.

Red-shanked douc

They bond by grooming each other. The colouring of their faces makes them look like they are wearing makeup.

Did you spot them all?

Owston's civit

A newborn civit weighs just 88 g (3 ounces) – that's about the same as a deck of cards! These civits are only be found in Vietnam, and small areas of the neighbouring countries of Laos and China, too.

Annamite striped rabbit

They have short tails, ears, and legs, and so they are not good at running.

The people helping

Tran Dang Hieu patrols the forest checking camera traps and gathering information about wildlife. He starts work at 7:30 am and travels up to 13 miles (20 km) a day on foot. When his patrols last a few days, he camps in the forest and sleeps in a hammock.

Bombs and chemicals caused great damage to the land during the Vietnam War. Since then, logging has destroyed even more forest. Today logging is illegal, but local communities still fell trees to sell the wood.

Indochinese tiger

The Indochinese tiger's stripes help it to blend in with the shadows in the rainforest.

Saola

The saola is one of the world's rarest and most mysterious animals. It is so elusive that it is often called the "Asian unicorn."

White-cheeked crested gibbon

It marks its territory by making sounds while moving around its patch. Its singing can be heard more than two miles away.

How you can help

Only buy sustainably made wood products. Look out for the Forest Stewardship Council (FSC) logo – you can find it on the back of this book. This means that the paper is made from trees grown in a well managed forest.

Edward's pheasant

These birds are only found in lowland forests in central Vietnam. It is believed that there are fewer than 250 left in the wild.

Crested argus

The tail of the male crested argus has only 12 feathers, but it can measure almost six feet long – that's longer than their body.

What can you see?

Yellow cowslip

Orange-tip butterfly

Red squirrel

UK

Dusk falls on an autumn evening at Kites Hill, England. In the woods, the beech trees glow like golden torches in the fading light. The only sounds are the wind in the leaves and the hoot of an owl. Suddenly, there's rustling on the woodland floor, then piglike grunts as a hedgehog appears from a pile of leaf-covered logs. It snuffles through the undergrowth searching for beetles, berries, and worms – it must fatten up as it will hibernate soon. As darkness descends, the cold air sharpens the smell of rotting vegetation. Throughout the night, the hedgehog will wander great distances looking for food. But it must be constantly on its guard, since hungry badgers will soon surface from their setts ...

The habitat

The United Kingdom's wild spaces include mountains, moorlands, marshes, and coast. Kites Hill in England was once part of a farm, but now its woods, meadows, scrub, and hedgerows are protected as a nature reserve.

The ancient beech woodlands of Kite's Hill are home to the endangered hedgehog and badger, as well as birdlife. Wildflowers flourish in the meadows and are vital for the survival of invertebrates such as bees, flies, beetles, spiders, moths, and butterflies.

Hedgerows

They are natural flood defences

Flowers

Lots of wildflowers carpet the grass of meadows in the summer

Wildflower meadows

This habitat is one of the rarest in the UK. Meadows are home to both grasses and flowers and are essential feeding sites for insects.

Tawny owls

The tawny owl is nocturnal. Its large eyes help it to hunt its prey in the dark.

Roe deer

Their coats are bright, rusty red in the summer, but turn to a dull grey in the winter.

Red fox

Male red foxes communicate with a barking sound. The sound a female makes is more like a scream.

Bumblebee

A bumblebee's wings beat more than 130 times per second. This helps to shake flowers until they release pollen. This is called buzz pollination.

Pyramidal orchid

The pyramid-shaped flowers of pyramidal orchids can range from pure white to deep magenta.

Did you spot them all?

Yellow cowslip

They smell faintly of apricots. You can make tea and wine from their flowers. Traditionally, cowslips were used to decorate May Day garlands and scattered outside churches on wedding days.

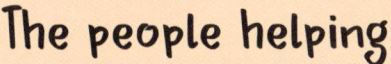

Common toad

You can tell the difference between the common toad and the common frog by looking at their skin. Common toads have warts on their skin, but common frogs don't.

Brown hare

They can run at speeds of up to 45 miles per hour when they are trying to escape predators.

The people helping

Jane Pointer was an English farmer. A trip to the forests of Belize inspired her to protect her own wilderness when she returned home. She donated her meadows and woodland – called Kites Hill – to the World Land Trust so they could guard it forever for wildlife.

Blue tit

These small birds typically only weigh around 11 g (⅓ ounce)!

Due to human activity, only 13% of the UK is still forested today. Wildlife is most threatened by habitat loss due to development such as building houses and roads. Hedgerows and trees have also been removed for agricultural growth.

Eurasian badger

Their homes are underground systems of burrows called setts which include sleeping chambers lined with leaves and grass. Families live together in them in clans.

European hedgehog

The weight of a European hedgehog can increase from ½ kg (1 lb) up to 2 kg (4 lb) in autumn, as they build up the fat reserves they need to hibernate through the winter.

How you can help

It might be tempting to be adventurous and stray from paths when out in the countryside. However, it's much better to stick to official walking routes to avoid accidentally disturbing animals or unnecessarily eroding the land.

Orange-tip butterfly

They may be called orange-tip butterflies but only the males of this species have orange tips on their wings. The females have black wing tips.

Red squirrel

They are the UK's native squirrel species. They have lived there for around ten thousand years! Despite this, they are much less common than the grey squirrel.

Belize

It's breakfast in the steamy rainforest of the Rio Bravo. A family of spider monkeys hang in a palm tree, munching on fruit. A baby clings to its mother as she holds on tight with her tail. Around them, the forest is a shadowy tangle of green. The roar of howler monkeys echoes around the trees, rising above the birdsong. On the forest floor, a tiny purple and green hummingbird zips between flowers, sipping nectar. A group of peccary are snuffling in the undergrowth, looking for food. Draped over a thick bough above them, another creature watches the scene carefully, also planning its next meal... a jaguar!

What can you see?

Ocellated turkey

Margay

Yellow-headed parrot

The habitat

Three quarters of Belize is covered in forest. This paradise is home to all of central America's five wildcats – jaguars, ocelots, pumas, jaguarundis, and margays.

In the far northwest of Belize, the Rio Bravo Conservation Area protects the forest and the creatures that live there. Today, nearly 10% of the country is protected for nature, and is connected with forests in Brazil and Guatemala.

Black orchid

This is the national flower of Belize. It flowers nearly all year round and grows on trees rather than directly out of the ground.

Baird's tapir

This is the national animal of Belize. The rhino is its closest relative.

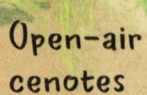

Open-air cenotes

These are caves that have completely collapsed

Yucatan black howler monkey

They are very noisy. Their howling sessions can last an hour and are as loud as a passing tube train!

Cenotes

Cenotes are caves that have collapsed in and been filled with groundwater and rainwater over time. The Mayans believed that cenotes were doorways to magical worlds!

Geoffroy's spider monkey

Every Geoffroy's spider monkey has a unique sound. This means that they can identify who is "talking."

Did you spot them all?

Ocellated turkey

Ocellated turkeys are only found in Mexico, Guatemala, and Belize. They have a shy nature, but they can be very noisy. Males and females have distinctive calls – males gobble and females cluck.

Mammee apple trees

They have large, apple-sized berries that humans and animals like to eat. Their leaves contain insecticides that can be used to protect young seedlings from insects.

Collared peccary

They walk on the middle two toes of their feet. Their other toes are higher up their legs, like a dog's dewclaw.

Logging and forest clearance for agriculture are the biggest threats to wildlife here. These activities are not allowed on the Rio Bravo reserve, but fires on neighbouring ranches can spread onto the reserve.

Hummingbird

These birds are the most agile on the planet. They can hover in mid-air by flapping their wings more than 50 times per second. They are the only birds that can fly backwards.

Jaguar

Their noises vary from a mew to grunts and growls, but they can also roar.

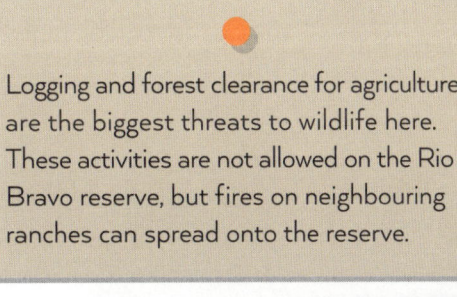

The people helping

Sometimes, illegal hunters start fires on purpose. The rangers on the Rio Bravo reserve are often the first responders to fires, so they have an important role to play in protecting the wildlife.

How you can help

Wildfires are often started accidentally. Always be careful with fire. Never play with matches or lighters. Always watch a campfire, and make sure it is completely out before leaving it.

Margay

Margays are very agile. Their hind feet can rotate 180 degrees, meaning that they are the only cat that can climb down a tree head first. Their long tails give them balance, and their large paws help them to grip trees.

Yellow-headed parrot

The talkative and boisterous yellow-headed parrot often bursts into song. They are highly sought after as pets, because they are able to imitate sounds and voices.

What can
you see?

Sitatunga

African pitta

African finfoot

Zambia

It's 6 am, and the sunrise is spreading its orangey-pink tendrils over Kasanka National Park. Sitatunga are already munching on the fresh grass that sprang up after the first rains of the wet season. Suddenly, the air is filled with flapping and chatter as millions of fruit bats start to appear from every direction. They blacken the dawn skies like a cloud of prehistoric pterodactyl. The bats are returning to roost after a night of foraging. They clamber noisily over one another, searching for a space to sleep on a tree branch. Occasionally, a bough snaps under their weight, followed by a squeal as the bats tumble to the ground. Finally, one by one, they settle, and silence descends again.

The habitat

Zambia is a land of forests, lakes, and floodplains. It also has spectacular waterfalls. Kasanka National Park provides a sanctuary for endangered wildlife, including the sitatunga, African elephants, and the African buffalo, as well as blue monkeys.

Kasanka National Park is a nesting and roosting site for endangered vultures, and it is the site of the largest mammal migration in the world. Between October and December every year, ten million straw-coloured fruit bats arrive to gorge on fruit while roosting in the forest.

Plants
Reeds and marsh plants grow here

River
The curves of a river are called meanders

Floodplain

This is the flat land next to a river that is often covered in water. A floodplain's ecosystem is usually more biodiverse than the ecosystem of the river.

Rattlepods
There are more than 600 species of rattlepods, and at least 500 of those are from Africa.

African buffalo
Their biggest enemies are lions.

Zebra
A zebra's stripes make them less obvious to their predators in reduced light. This type of camouflage is called disruptive colouration.

African elephant
They are the world's largest land mammal. They need to eat almost constantly and cover great distances to find enough food.

Did you spot them all?

Sitatunga
These swamp-dwelling antelopes are excellent swimmers. They will even submerge themselves completely underwater to hide from predators.

Sausage tree

The fruit looks just like... a sausage! Each fruit can weigh more than 13 kg (28 lb).

The people helping

Benson Bweupe and Kalaba Kalassa are rangers in Kasanka National Park. They protect animals from poachers and rescue those that have been injured in traps. It is a dangerous job, because elephants can become aggressive when they feel threatened.

Zambia's population is growing, which has led to local communities chopping down trees to collect honey and make charcoal for fuel.

Blue monkey

Its tail and body are about the same length.

Fruit bat

Each bat can consume twice its body weight in food each night.

Wattled crane

Their wattle is like a turkey's but their body is like a small flamingo's.

African leopard

They can leap 6 metres (19 ft) forward through the air and run at up to 58 mph (93 kph).

How you can help

Many of us enjoy seeing bats flit across the evening sky. Put up a bat box in your garden to give these night creatures somewhere safe to roost, raise their pups, and sleep during the day.

African pitta

This shy bird likes to hide and can remain motionless for long periods of time. Although they are very brightly coloured, they are hard to spot on the dense forest floor.

African finfoot

They have a neon orange bill, legs, and feet. They are reclusive and prefer to live in secluded areas where the trees are thick, so they can easily hide out of sight.

Guatemala

It's midnight in the Sierra Santa Cruz mountains. In the rainforest, the humid darkness trills with the sound of crickets. The moon gleams brightly overhead, and its silvery beams pierce through the canopy. Here, the night creatures are beginning to stir. Frogs crawl from their leafy hideouts, calling for mates and searching for food, while vampire bats flit through the air. Two orange orbs glisten in the darkness – a silent, stealthy margay is hunting for prey. She moves with the ease of an acrobat, running along boughs and leaping between trees. Suddenly, she spots a snake on the forest floor. In a flash, she's descending headfirst down a tree trunk and getting ready to pounce...

What can you see?

Chinamococh stream frog

Merendon palm pit viper

Long-limbed salamander

The habitat

Guatemala is a land of lush landscapes, towering volcanoes, and Mayan ruins. Its habitats range from rivers, wetlands, mangroves, and lagoons to sky-high cloud forests, dry forests, and rainforests.

Trees

The highest level of trees is called the emergent layer

Forest floor

This is the lowest and darkest part of the rainforest

Tropical rainforest

Rainforests have tall trees and a lot of rainfall. They have four layers that all work together so that a variety of animals and plants can live there.

Cacao tree

Guatemala is said to be the birthplace of chocolate. It is made of the roasted seeds from the fruit of the cacao tree.

Red-eyed tree frog

This frog is usually green and blends in with the rainforest leaves, but it can change its colour depending on its mood.

The Sierra Santa Cruz Reserve protects the rainforest home of rare species, from endemic frogs and vultures, to scarab beetles and big cats, such as the agile margay.

Jackson's climbing salamander

This salamander's nickname is the "golden wonder" because of its colour.

Vampire bat

These bats usually roost in caves and tree hollows. They can also be found in old wells, mine shafts, and abandoned buildings.

Keel-billed motmot

These birds like to sit very still, like statues.

Did you spot them all?

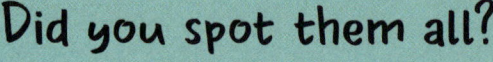

Chinamococh stream frog

These frogs come out at night to hunt and mate. If a pair mates successfully, the female can lay around 150 eggs in the same night.

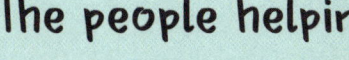

Tamandua

These small anteaters scare predators away with their horrible smell, which they release from a gland at the base of their tail.

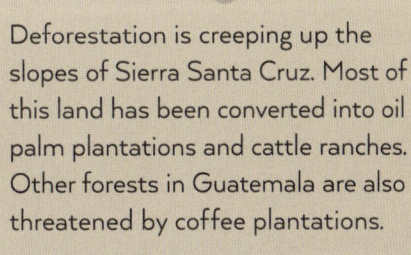

Blackburnian warbler

This bird migrates from North America to South America for the winter.

Deforestation is creeping up the slopes of Sierra Santa Cruz. Most of this land has been converted into oil palm plantations and cattle ranches. Other forests in Guatemala are also threatened by coffee plantations.

White nun orchid

This is the national flower of Guatemala. It symbolizes peace, beauty, and art.

Copan stream frog

They jump by quickly pushing out both of their back legs at the same time. This is called "saltation."

The people helping

Ricardo Caal protects one of Guatemala's rainforest and wetlands reserves. He patrols by foot and canoe to look out for hunters and people cutting down trees. He also works with local communities to help ensure the future of the reserve.

How you can help

The number of frogs and toads in the UK and Europe is declining because of habitat loss, particularly ponds. You can help by adding a mini-pond in your garden. Also avoid using pesticides and slug pellets that can make garden pests unsafe for amphibians to eat.

Merendon palm pit viper

These snakes have a pit organ on both sides of their head. The pit organ senses heat and so the vipers can detect their prey even when there is no light.

Long-limbed salamander

North, Central, and South America are home to more species of salamander than the rest of the world put together. The long-limbed salamander was first discovered in the 1970s but then wasn't seen again until 2014.

Cameroon

Deep in a forest in Cameroon, above the chirrup of insects and birds, there's a mysterious sound of hammering and cracking. Beneath the shadowy tangle of trees and vines, a patch of forest floor is littered with broken walnut shells. The noise is coming from above. Perched on a thick bough high in an African walnut tree, a female chimpanzee is busy at work. She pulls a fat, green walnut from a branch and bashes it open with a big stone before cramming the insides into her mouth. Sitting nearby, her youngster watches carefully before trying to copy, tapping on a nut with a twig. Remembering her infant, the mother stops and passes him some food.

What can you see?

African grey parrot

Congo clawless otter

Grey-necked rock fowl

The habitat

Cameroon's hot and humid climate means much of the country is covered in rainforest, but this is becoming more and more fragmented.

Ground vegetation

More sunlight helps it to grow

Tree stumps

Slowly regrowing after being logged

Secondary forest

These are forests that have been disturbed by human activity. The canopy provides less cover, the trees are smaller, and fewer plants and animals live in them.

Deng Deng National Park protects many vulnerable species. African forest elephants, chimpanzees, hippopotamuses, African grey parrots, and the critically endangered western lowland gorilla all call the park home.

African forest elephant

It is smaller than the African savannah elephant. Its tusks are straighter and point downwards.

Red-hot poker

Also called torch lillies, these plants usually grow in swamps.

Chimpanzee

They are one of the few species known to use sticks and stones as tools for foraging and feeding. They are highly intelligent and one of our closest relatives in the animal kingdom.

Western lowland gorilla

They are the smallest of the gorilla species. They build nests to sleep in at night and for their midday nap.

Did you spot them all?

African grey parrot

These birds are hunted in the wild to supply the illegal pet trade. Parrots are well known for being able to mimic sounds when they are kept as pets, but they are not known to do this in the wild.

Walnut tree

They are often planted by cocoa farmers, as they provide shade for cocoa orchards.

The people helping

Local people are helping to create community forests and wildlife corridors between protected areas. Many are also turning away from poaching and logging to nature-friendly jobs such as bee-keeping, cassava farming, and cattle rearing.

More than half a million acres of forest are cleared every year in Cameroon – that's about the same size as West Sussex. The remaining forest is very fragmented, which affects species movement.

Hippopotamus

The name means "river horse" in Greek. Their nostrils and eyes are high on their head, making them well adapted to life in the water.

Kordofan giraffe

They drink water only once every few days and get the rest of their liquid from food.

West African crocodile

This species is smaller and friendlier than the Nile crocodile that it was confused with for many years.

How you can help

Woods and forests are crucial for human health and happiness, as well as providing a home for wildlife. You can help nature and fight climate change by planting trees.

Congo clawless otter

These otters like to live alone in mountain streams and lowland swamps. They are strong swimmers, although they spend more time on land than other otters. Their dark coats help to camouflage them in swamps.

Grey-necked rock fowl

They breed and build their nests in caves and on rock faces. They prefer to have overhanging rocks above to protect the nest, and a seasonal river below.

Argentina

It's September in Argentinian Patagonia, and hundreds of magellanic penguins are guarding their burrows. Many are dug beneath bushes to protect the eggs from hungry foxes and the clumsy feet of guanaco and rhea. Above the crashing waves, the raucous penguins sound like a cross between a braying donkey and a honking goose. The males and females take turns to waddle to the sea to hunt for food. In the water live the whales, dolphins, and seals that also call this region home. Here, on the sands of Estancia La Esperanza is where the Patagonian Steppe meets the Atlantic Ocean, and the penguins have returned to their birthplace to hatch and raise their young.

What can you see?

Patagonian mara

Rufous-collared sparrow

Darwin's slipper flower

The habitat

Argentina's landscapes range from Andean peaks and the high plateaus of the puna, to the lowland plains of the Chaco and grasslands of the Pampas. Patagonia, in the south, has large areas of steppe.

The Estancia La Esperanza reserve is home to wildlife adapted to the region's strong winds, extreme temperatures, and dry conditions. Foxes, penguins, pumas, and armadillos all live here. Birdlife includes the burrowing owl and birds of prey.

Magellanic penguin

They can dive to depths of 100 metres (328 ft). Their feathers have a waterproof coating of oil to help keep them warm.

Lesser rhea

The lesser rhea's body is about the same size as a sheep. They run in a zigzag pattern when fleeing from predators.

Trees

Steppe environments don't have many trees

Burrows

Penguin burrows are found close to the sea

Southern elephant seal

They are the world's largest seal species. The average weight for a male is 3 tonnes.

Desert steppe

This is the scrubland between the sea and the mountains. It's dry and cold, and windy all year round.

Buzzard eagles

Despite their large size, buzzard eagles are usually timid.

El rincon stream frog

They can be found in hot springs. These help them to survive in Argentina's often freezing temperatures.

Did you spot them all?

Patagonian mara

The Patagonian mara is a type of rodent. Their closest living relative is the guinea pig. Maras live together in communal burrows. Female maras are able to identify their own infants by their smell.

Pygmy armadillo

They are not often seen, because they spend a lot of time underground to escape extreme temperatures.

Wildlife in Estancia La Esperanza is threatened by development. Habitat is being destroyed for oil exploration; cattle ranching; and sugar cane, tobacco, and soya plantations.

Blue whale

It is the largest animal on the planet. They can weigh up to 200 metric tonnes. Their tongues alone can weigh as much as an elephant, and their hearts can weigh as much as a car!

Burrowing owl

They nest underground, typically using burrows that have been dug and then abandoned by other animals.

Cockspur coral tree

The cockspur coral tree is the national tree and flower of Argentina. The red flowers even have their own annual National Day on 22 November!

The people helping

Axel Kuchaska patrols Estancia La Esperanza reserve to look out for poachers, monitor camera traps, and restore vegetation after wildfires. He helped care for an injured buzzard eagle before it was released back into the wild.

How you can help

If it's not far, don't use the car! Our need for oil and other fossil fuels causes habitat destruction as well as greenhouse gas emissions. Traffic also causes air pollution which is unhealthy for humans and wildlife.

Rufous-collared sparrow

This species is found across South America, but their call changes depending on where they live. In some places the birds trill, and in others they whistle, and in some places they do a combination of both.

Darwin's slipper flower

These plants are said to have been discovered by the famous English naturalist Charles Darwin. The flowers look like little orange penguins. They are best suited to cold climates.

What can you see?

Snake-necked turtle

Green-headed tanager

Poison dart frog

Brazil

In the Guapiaçu Reserve in eastern Brazil, a caiman ploughs silently through a lake, slicing through the lily pads and reeds. Only its head and back are visible, cresting the green-flecked water. A heron poses like a statue in the shallows, and vultures patrol the skies overhead. Beyond these wetlands, the emerald green forest continues up to the distant mountain tops. A flock of white egret floats by and settles in tree roosts close to the water. Eventually, the caiman reaches an island in the middle of the lake. It crawls onto the shore, startling a group of beached capybara. They stop moving instantly and eye their new companion nervously.

The habitat

The dense rainforests of the Amazon, the flooded wetlands of the Pantanal, and the dry grasslands of the Cerrado, make Brazil the most biodiverse country in the world. The Atlantic Forest – the second largest rainforest in South America – once stretched all the way along South America's east coast.

The Guapiaçu Reserve protects an area of the Atlantic Forest. Here, wetlands have been restored and native trees have been planted. The area is home to rare wildlife, including the central humming frog, the multi-coloured green headed tanager, and the southern woolly spider monkey.

Lowland tapir

They use their long noses to grab trees when on land and as a snorkel when swimming.

Capybara

Their teeth grow throughout their entire life. Eating grass and plants wears them down.

Sea

Forests that are influenced by the sea are said to have "high oceanicity."

Brown-throated three-toed sloth

They sleep for up to 20 hours a day! They have long claws that allow them to hang from tree branches.

Coastal rainforest

This habitat is found only in places that are influenced by the sea. The temperatures in coastal rainforests do not change much throughout the year, and they have high levels of rainfall.

White egret

The white egret's neck is longer than its body.

Did you spot them all?

Snake-necked turtle

They are endemic to the Atlantic Forest of south-east Brazil. They live in cold upland rivers and streams. They like to bask in the warmth of the sun and so look for spots where there are gaps in the cover of the rainforest.

Woolly spider monkey

The hands and tails of the woolly spider monkey can hold onto tree branches, making them very agile.

Central humming frog

This humming frog is endemic to Brazil. Humming frogs get their name from the noise that males make during breeding season.

The Atlantic Forest is one of the most threatened forest regions in the world. Most of it has been cleared for agriculture and pasture. Cattle grazing has led to runoff that has damaged water quality.

Toco toucan

They rest their beaks on their backs and fold their tails over their head when they sleep.

Capped heron

They have blue lores. The lores are where the beak meets the face.

Spectacled caiman

If an environment becomes too harsh, spectacled caimans dig into the mud and estivate – this is a form of hibernation.

The people helping

Local people work at the reserve's tree nursery. They collect seeds from the forest floor and grow them in the nursery. They then plant the seedlings to reforest bare pastures with native tree species.

How you can help

Autumn is the ideal time to collect tree seeds, such as acorns. You can grow these into seedlings and replant them in the woods. Trees grown from local seeds are well suited to local conditions, such as soil, climate, and seasonal patterns.

Green-headed tanager

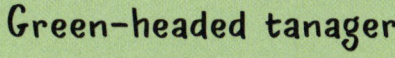

These birds are very bright – they are usually a combination of six different colours! Other types of tanagers have complicated calls, but the green-headed tanager simply chirps.

Poison dart frog

Instead of camouflage, poison dart frogs have brightly coloured skin to warn other animals that they aren't safe to eat. Their skin secretes poison that can paralyze, or even kill, predators!

Colombia

The midday sun beats down on the Magdalena River as a fisherman catches dinner for his family. His boat is shaded by the leaves of the mangrove trees that grow up from below the water along the river bank. Nearby, a turtle basks on a floating log. Suddenly, the fisherman spies a large, dark shape gliding towards him and freezes. Could it be a crocodile? Then, a grey nose breaks through the water's surface and sucks in a breath of air before sinking down again. The fisherman lets out a sigh of relief and chuckles. It's just a manatee! He now sees that her calf is swimming alongside her, too. The mother gently pushes her baby up to breathe. Then they both disappear and paddle away, grazing from the riverbed as they go.

What can you see?

Lozano's salamander

Golden poison frog

Magdalena river turtle

The habitat

Colombia has mountains, mangrove swamps, desert scrub, savannahs, and rainforests. Colombia's main river is the Magdalena River in the Magdalena Valley.

The El Silencio Reserve protects an area of pristine rainforest and wetlands. It is home to both big and small creatures, including jaguars and the rare Lozano salamander. Turtles, piranhas, crocodiles, and electric eels live in the waterways.

Tropical tree

Mangroves can't survive in freezing temperatures and only grow near the equator

White-fronted capuchin

They have been seen using tools, such as cups made out of leaves.

Northern screamer

They are wading birds but prefer to be on land.

Electric eel

They can't breathe underwater, so they rise to the water's surface to take in air.

Roots

Fish can hide from predators in the mangrove's roots

Macarenia clavigera

This aquatic plant only grows in Colombia's Caño Cristales river. For a few months each year, it turns the riverbed into a spectacular rainbow of red, yellow, green, blue, and black.

Mangrove forest

Mangrove forests are made up of trees that live between water and land. They are easy to identify, because the tree's roots can be seen.

American crocodile

The sex of baby American crocodiles is determined by the temperature their eggs are incubated at. Cooler conditions produce females, and warmer temperatures produce males.

Did you spot them all?

Lozano's salamander

This salamander looks a little bit like a sausage and is endemic to Colombia. Salamanders cannot hear sound, and they don't make any noise either.

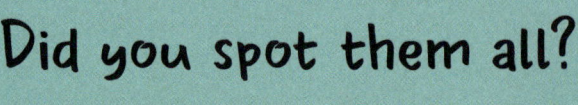

Devil's snare

They do not strangle like the plant in the famous magical books. However, they are very poisonous. They are used by Indigenous communities for sacred ceremonies.

Cattle ranching has replaced most of the original forest. Palm oil plantations and mining are also destroying habitats as well as heavily polluting the environment.

Red-bellied piranha

These freshwater fish live in rivers and lakes rather than the sea.

White-footed tamarin

They spend most of their time in the forest canopy, where they use all four of their limbs to move around.

Blue-billed curassow

When they were first discovered, blue-billed curassows were named Prince Albert curassows, after Queen Victoria's husband.

West Indian manatee

They are often called "sea cows." They can stay submerged under water for 20 minutes before coming up for air.

The people helping

Volunteers from local villages have trained to become "turtle guardians." During nesting season, they patrol beaches to protect eggs from tourists and poachers. They also raise awareness about conservation in their schools and communities.

How you can help

Look out for *Puro* tea and coffee in shops. Buying their products helps fund rangers and camera traps for Colombia's conservation projects, as well as ensuring that local growers are paid fairly for their crops.

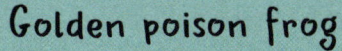

Golden poison frog

They are believed to be the most poisonous vertebrate on earth! Each tiny frog has enough poison in its body to kill ten humans.

Magdalena river turtle

They only live in freshwater and like to bask on logs. They eat fallen fruit, seeds, vegetation, insects, and aquatic invertebrates, such as mussels and snails.

What can you see?

Horned marsupial frog

Pampas cat

White-necked parakeet

Ecuador

High in Ecuador's Chocó Forest, an enormous nest lies in the branches of a towering Brazil nut tree. It's so wide that a human could sleep in it. Sitting in the nest is a screeching, fluffy, white eaglet the size of a turkey. Its mother, a harpy eagle, perches on a nearby bough, scanning the forest below. Their tree is the tallest in the area and rises above a tapestry of leafy crowns of many colours and shapes, including palm trees splayed out like flower petals. When she finally spies a sloth lazily munching on leaves, she drops from her perch and dives at her prey with lightning speed.

The habitat

Ecuador straddles part of the Andes mountains and occupies part of the Amazon River basin. Along the coast, the Chocó Forest lies between the Pacific Ocean and the Andes.

The diversity of Ecuador's habitats makes it one of the most biodiverse countries in the world, with thousands of bird and plant species.

Trees

The treeline is the edge of the habitat where trees are able to grow

Mountain

The snow line is the lowest point at which there can be permanent snow cover

Kinkajou

They usually eat fruit and insects, but they are also called "honey bears," because they raid beehives and use their long, skinny tongues to slurp honey.

Magnolia canandeana

The magnolia canandeana species was recently discovered in Ecuador, and only three trees have been found.

Andean condor

The Andean condor is the largest flying bird in South America. They are the raptors with the longest wingspan in the world – it measures more than 3 metres (10 ft).

Páramo

Páramo is found at high altitudes between the treeline and the snowline. It is very important for supplying water to local communities.

Harpy eagle

Female harpy eagles are almost twice as big as male harpy eagles.

Did you spot them all?

Horned marsupial frog

They live up in the forest canopy, but they also like to be near water. The males call from high trees with a loud "bop" sound. These frogs were thought to be extinct in Ecuador until they were seen again in 2018.

Chocó toucan

Their beaks might look heavy, but they are actually hollow and light.

Fausto, Luis, Santiago, and Jesús Recalde are four brothers who work as wildlife rangers. After a bad rainy season with landslides that destroyed houses and roads, they had to clear fallen trees and rebuild paths into the Cerro Candelaria Reserve.

Tik tik rainfrog

These frogs are smaller than a thumbnail!

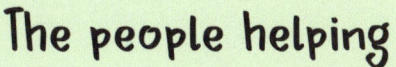

The greatest threat to wildlife is habitat loss due to Ecuador's growing human population. There is deforestation for logging and land clearance for animal pasture and crops, such as banana and sugar cane.

Brown-headed spider monkey

Unlike other spider monkeys, the brown headed spider monkey doesn't have any white markings.

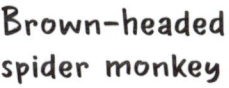

Heliconia

This plant also goes by the name "parrot flower," because the leaves look like beaks.

Hoffmann's two-toed sloth

They move so slowly that algae grows on their coats. This gives them a green tinge that helps them to blend in with their forest surroundings.

How you can help

Across the world, about one third of the food produced for humans gets wasted. This uses up natural resources like water and energy and contributes to climate change. You can help by using up all your food before going shopping again. Eat leftovers for lunch or make banana bread from overripe bananas that would otherwise go to waste!

Pampas cat

They look a lot like a big domestic housecat. The colour of a pampas cat's coat varies depending on where it lives. High in the Andes, it is usually grey, but their coats are longer and yellow-brown in colour in Argentina.

White-necked parakeet

These parakeets are usually found in small, noisy flocks flitting between trees. White-necked parakeets need minerals to help them digest their food, which they can get from the clay in cliff faces.

Bolivia

In the Beni savannah of northern Bolivia, a small, forested island is alive with the sound of ear-shattering squawks. The dark green palm trees appear bejewelled with turquoise and gold. A flock of fifty macaws – many in playful mating pairs – feed on fat bunches of fruit. From their noisy, treetop feast, palm seeds drop to the ground, where a peccary is picnicking on the forest floor. It's the rainy season, and what was once a sea of golden grassland stretching for hundreds of miles is now a patchwork of forested islands. It's here that giant anteaters snuffle for termites, prowling wolves howl at dusk, and the jaguar stalks its prey.

What can you see?

Cock-tailed tyrant

Black-masked finch

Catesby's snail sucker

The habitat

One third of Bolivia lies in the Andes mountains while the rest is lowland plains, savannah, swamps, and tropical forests. The Beni savannah is twice the size of Portugal and has several habitats, including tropical grassland, forest islands, and marshy wetlands.

The Barba Azul Nature Reserve protects the world's last remaining blue-throated macaws and the magnificent wildlife sharing their home.

Trees

Montacu palms here are between 60 and 90 years old

Babassu palm tree

Babassu oil comes from the nuts of the babassu palm tree. The tree's fruit is used in cosmetics, and its leaves are used to make roofs and paper.

White-lipped peccary

They live in big herds. There can be more than 300 individual peccaries in a herd.

Forested islands

These islands are created when rainfall and melted snow from the Andes mountains flood the savannah.

Bolivian river dolphin

Their pink colour is because of the algae they eat. They are very playful and can swim upside down!

Capybara

They can stay underwater for up to five minutes. This comes in handy when they need to hide from predators!

Did you spot them all?

Cock-tailed tyrant

These quiet birds barely make any sound. One of the ways they hunt is by sallying. This means that they dash and catch their prey in mid-air before taking it back to a perch to eat.

Monkey tail cactus

The spines of the monkey tail cactus look soft like hair, but beware – they're not! These plants survive on the moisture in the air.

Ipê tree

The ipê tree blooms in colours from white through to pink, lavender, and red. It is known for its resistance to fire, which is comparable to concrete and steel.

Tropical grassland is one of the most threatened habitats in the world. In South America, savannah habitats are under constant pressure to be converted to enormous soya bean farms and cattle ranches.

Guanaco

Newborn guanaco are able to run shortly after birth. Mothers and babies often make humming noises to contact each other.

Blue-throated macaw

These birds were believed to be extinct until 1992. It's estimated that there are only 250-300 left in the wild.

Common potoo

The potoo can sense movement, even with its eyes closed!

The people helping

Miguel Martínez and Jesús Arauz are wildlife rangers. One of their jobs is creating and maintaining firebreaks. Firebreaks help to prevent fires from spreading and causing more damage and devastation.

How you can help

The meat and dairy industries contribute a lot to pollution, climate change, and deforestation. When we produce meat, we're using up valuable land and crops to rear animals. One way to help is by trying to eat less meat and dairy.

Black-masked finch

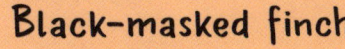

A bird's beak has two parts. The top part is called the maxilla, and the bottom part is called the mandible. Black-masked finches have a bright yellow mandible. Humans have mandibles, too – it's our lower jaw.

Catesby's snail sucker

These nonvenomous snakes are named after the creatures they eat – snails. Snail suckers have long teeth that they use to grab the snail. They then use their lower teeth to pull the snail out of its shell.

What can you see?

Great hornbill

Bonnet macaque

Elephant foot yam

India

In the Western Ghats mountains of southern India, a baby elephant is stuck in the mud after the monsoon rain. At a few days old, he's still a little wobbly on his legs. Hearing the calf's anxious calls, his mother has stopped beside him. She wraps her trunk around his stomach and gently pulls him free. The rest of the herd – six females and their young – are waiting. Seeing that all is well, the matriarch trumpets loudly, and they set off again, lumbering through the forest. There's a flash of purple and red as a giant squirrel darts up a tree to avoid the herd's wrinkled feet.

The habitat

It might be hard to believe that India's many distinct habitats can all exist in the same country. The Himalayas – the world's highest mountain range – and the wettest place on earth can both be found here.

Dry season

Trees shed their leaves

Monsoon season

Leaves begin to regrow

Monsoon forest

This type of forest has a long dry season of six months or more. This is followed by a season of heavy rain.

The Thirunelli-Kudrakote animal corridor is crucial for connecting fragments of habitat. India is home to the largest population of Asian elephants in the world. It is also the only place where both lions and tigers live.

Dhole

They are also known as "whistling dogs" because of the sound they make when trying to reunite their pack.

Indian leopard

Their rosettes are larger than the rosettes of other subspecies of leopard.

Gaur

Male gaur "sing" to get the attention of females. The sound gets lower the longer they sing.

Indian giant squirrel

They are one of the largest squirrels on the planet! Instead of storing nuts and seeds underground, they stash them in the treetops.

Did you spot them all?

Great hornbill

Hornbills build their nests in holes in trees. The female hornbill stays with her eggs inside the hole, and covers the entrance with food and twigs to keep the nest safe. The male then feeds the female through a small gap.

Symplocos mohananii

This recently discovered plant has white flowers that usually open during the night. New wild things are being found all the time!

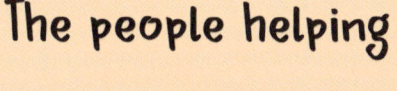

The people helping

Many villages in India have an elephant early warning system. Rangers track herd movements and send text messages to people if the animals will come through their area. This has reduced the number of elephant-human conflicts, when people or elephants can get hurt or killed.

Humans are the biggest threat to wildlife survival here. Elephants are killed for their tusks, while tigers are poached for meat, medicine, and to be kept as pets.

Bengal tiger

Tigers are the largest of the big cat species. The other big cats are lions, jaguars, leopards, and snow leopards. Bengal tigers can grow up to three metres (10 ft) long.

Banyan tree

Their many roots grow down from their branches. This makes them appear like lots of trees, when it is, in fact, just one tree.

Asian elephants

They usually live in groups of six or seven related females, and the oldest is their leader. Male elephants live alone.

How you can help

Never buy products made from animal parts, such as ivory. Animals are illegally poached for these products.

Bonnet macaque

These monkeys can often be found near human settlements. They steal food from houses, markets, and even from temples where it has been left as a religious offering.

Elephant foot yam

Elephant foot yams have a horrible scent. When they bloom, they generate heat. The heat and smell attract flies to pollinate them.

Paraguay

Night has fallen in the Paraguayan Chaco, and the darkness hums with a chorus of insects. The day was as hot as a furnace, but now it's cooling quickly. From a hole in the pink, dusty ground, a twitching nose appears. An armadillo climbs out of her burrow and sniffs the night air. Catching a scent, she begins weaving between the cacti and spiky bromeliads. A black and red snake swiftly slithers into the bristly undergrowth to avoid becoming supper. But he doesn't need to worry tonight – the armadillo has other plans. Arriving at a tall mound of dried mud, she balances on her tail and back legs and starts digging with her fierce front claws. Orange termites erupt from the mud like lava from a volcano, and she laps them up with her long tongue.

What can you see?

Green racer

White-eared puffbird

Oncilla

The habitat

Paraguay's habitats range from the dry forests and grasslands of the Chaco, to the swamps and wetlands of the Pantanal. The Gran Chaco is a dry, flat, sparsely populated area. It has been called the last great wilderness.

The Chaco-Pantanal Reserve is a hotspot of biodiversity. Thousands of migratory birds stop here, and the reserve is also home to the "Three Giants" – the giant anteater, the giant armadillo, and the giant otter.

Coraline frog

It lives in burrows and comes out at night to hunt. Its prey is smaller frogs.

Chaco tortoise

The Chaco tortoise is medium-sized, but its closest living relative is the Galápagos tortoise – the biggest living tortoise in the world!

Plants

Xerophytes are plants that can survive with only a little bit of water

Coral snake

Most coral snakes are tricoloured – that means that their skin is three colours.

Giant anteater

They walk on their knuckles. They're not the only animals to do this – gorillas do it too.

Dry Chaco

The dry Chaco only gets a small amount of rainfall. The forests here are scrub forests with cacti, grasses, and shrubs.

Giant armadillo

They live in savanna or forests close to water. When they are scared, they will run towards the nearest hole or try to burrow into the ground.

Did you spot them all?

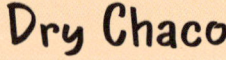

Green racer

Just like most reptiles, the green racer snake is oviparous. This means that the female lays an egg, and the embryos grow inside the egg rather than inside her body, like a human embryo would.

Chaco owl

Their call is more like a frog's croak than the soft "twit twoo" noise you might think of.

The people helping

Lourdes Matoso is a ranger in Paraguay's Chaco-Pantanal region, where the dry forests meet the wetlands. She photographs wildlife to add to the register of species that is being built. She also sets up and monitors camera traps and maintains the trails.

Land clearance for cattle ranching and soya production is the biggest threat to wildlife survival. The Gran Chaco has one of the highest deforestation rates in the world. On average, an area of forest the size of 1,500 football pitches is destroyed here every day.

Maned wolf

The maned wolf has a mane on its neck which stands upright when it senses danger.

Drunken tree

It has a swollen trunk which is adapted to retain water in the dry Chaco habitat.

Azara's night monkey

Although they are called a night monkey, they are active both during the day and at night.

How you can help

Most of the soya grown on the Gran Chaco is used to feed pigs, cows, and chickens for our food. Deforestation of the region has an impact on climate change. You can help by eating less meat and dairy products, even if that's just once a week.

White-eared puffbird

Puffbirds have short tails and their heads often look too big for their bodies. They are "sit and wait" feeders, which means that they catch their prey by surprise.

Oncilla

The oncilla is nicknamed the "little tiger cat" because of its markings. However, some oncillas are completely black, and they live in the denser parts of forests. Oncillas are also good swimmers, which is unusual for a cat.

Glossary

Have you seen any new words during your adventures? Use this glossary to learn their meaning.

algae
An organism usually found in water that can perform photosynthesis

amphibian
Small vertebrates that can only survive in water or in a moist environment

biodiversity
How much variety can be found among the things that live in a place

canopy
The second highest level of a forest. It is thick with leaves and branches and protects the lower levels of the forest from rain, sun, and wind.

carnivore
An animal that eats other animals, or a plant that eats small animals, such as insects

cassava
A type of vegetable that has a nutty taste and looks quite similar to a sweet potato

conservation
Protecting the world's natural resources so they continue to exist

deforestation
When forests or land with lots of trees on it are cleared on purpose

dormant
When an animal or plant stops being active, like it is asleep. Animals and plants do this to survive difficult conditions.

ecosystem
How all the organisms and the environment in a geographic area work together. Ecosystems have living parts – such as plants and animals – and non-living parts, such as rocks and the climate.

endangered
A species that is at risk of extinction

endemic
A plant or animal that can only be found in one place

extinct
A species that no longer exists, such as dinosaurs

fell
Cutting down

fossil fuels
Material that forms underground and is extracted by drilling. Humans then burn fossil fuels to release energy. Natural gas is a fossil fuel that we use to power household items such as boilers and kitchen hobs.

fragmented
Something that was once large and continuous but is now broken into smaller, more separate parts

fresh water
Any water that occurs naturally and doesn't have a lot of salt in it, such as rivers and lakes

habitat
The place that animals, plants, and other organisms call home

herbivore
An animal that usually only eats plant material, such as leaves

invertebrate
A cold-blooded animal that doesn't have a backbone

logging
The process of cutting and moving trees so that they can be transported somewhere else

mammal
A vertebrate animal whose young are fed with milk from the mother's mammary glands

matriarch
A female that is in charge of a family or group

migrate
Moving from one place to another, usually when seasons change

mineral lick
A place that animals visit to lick to get the nutrients they can't get from the food they eat

native
A person, animal, or plant that originally comes from a place and occurs there naturally

nocturnal
Something that happens or is active at night time

plankton
Organisms that are carried along by the tide or currents in water

plantation
A large estate that usually grows and farms only one crop

poaching
Illegally hunting or catching wild animals on land where this isn't allowed

pollinator
An animal that moves pollen from a male flower to a female flower

predator
An animal that naturally preys on other animals

raptor
A bird of prey that mostly hunts and eats vertebrates

reptile
Vertebrates that are cold-blooded

resin
A thick, sticky fluid that plants produce to protect themselves when they are hurt

roost
A perch that birds will return to and rest on at night

runoff
Water that drains from an area of land

species
A type of animal or plant

succulent
The thick leaves or stems of a plant that are adapted to store water

temperate
A place where the climate is mild

trafficking
Poaching and trading of protected animals and plants

venomous
An animal that can inject venom when it bites or stings

vertebrate
Any animal that has a backbone inside its body

Animal index

Invertebrates

 **Blue-ringed octopus**
33, 34

 **Bullet ant**
8-9, 10

 **Bumblebee**
42

 **Coral**
32-33, 34

 **Electric eel**
70

 **Giant clam**
32-33, 35

 **Monarch butterfly**
16-17, 19

 **Mountain alcon blue butterfly**
23

 **Orange-tip butterfly**
40-41, 43

 **Orchid mantis**
12-13, 15

 **Pyrops intricatus**
12-13, 14

Sea anemone
32-33, 35

 **Termites**
84

 **Venezuelan poodle moth**
9, 11

 **Tomares romanov butterfly**
20-21, 22

Fish

 **Blacktip reef shark**
34

 **Clownfish**
35

 **Bargibant's pygmy seahorse**
33, 35

 **Red-bellied piranha**
68-69, 71

 **Tiger tail seahorse**
34

Reptiles

 **American crocodile**
68, 70

 **Armenin viper**
23

 **Catesby's snail sucker**
76-77, 79

 **Chaco tortoise**
86

 **Coral snake**
85, 86

 **Green iguana**
8, 10

 **Green racer**
84-85, 86.

 **Green sea turtle**
32, 34

 **Magdalena river turtle**
69, 71

 **Merendon palm pit viper**
53, 55

 **Peruvian coral snake**
29, 31

 **Reticulated python**
38

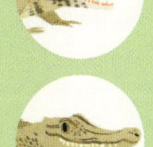 **Snake-necked turtle**
64, 66

 **Spectacled caiman**
64, 67

 **West African crocodile**
59

Amphibian

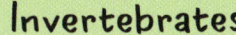 **Bell's false brook salamander**
16-17, 18

 **Central humming frog**
67

 Chinamococh
stream frog
52-53, 54

 Common toad
43

 Copan stream frog
53, 55

 Coraline frog
86

 El rincon stream frog
62

 Golden poison frog
69, 71

 Horned marsupial frog
72-73, 74

 Jackson's climbing
salamander
53, 54

 Long-limbed
salamander
53, 55

 Lozano's salamander
68-69, 70

 Poison dart frog
64, 67

Red-eyed tree frog
53, 54

Tik tik rain frog
75

Birds

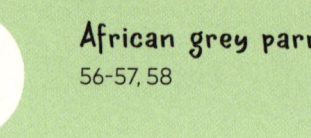 African finfoot
48, 51

 African grey parrot
56-57, 58

 African pitta
48, 51

 American flamingo
9, 11

 Bearded vulture
21, 22

 Bearded
wood-partridge
16-17, 19

 Black-masked finch
76-77, 79

 Blackburnian warbler
52, 55

 Blue-billed curassow
71

 Blue-throated macaw
76-77, 79

Blue tit
41, 43

Blue-crowned parakeet
8-9, 11

 Bumblebee
hummingbird
18

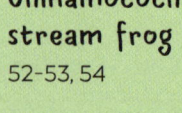 Burrowing owl
63

 Buzzard eagle
60-61, 62-63

 Capped heron
64, 67

 Chaco owl
85, 87

 Choco toucan
73, 75

 Cock-tailed tyrant
76-77, 78

 Common potoo
79

 Crested argus
36-37, 39

 Crowned hawk eagle
24-25, 27

 Edward's pheasant
36, 39

 Emerald toucanet
16, 19

European roller
21, 23

Great hornbill
80, 82

 Green-headed tanager
64, 67

Grey-necked rock fowl
57, 59

Red-faced parrot
28, 30

Harpy eagle
73, 74

Rufous-collared sparrow
60-61, 63

African buffalo
48, 50

Hummingbird
47

Sharpe's longclaw
24-25, 27

African elephant
49, 50

Jackson's widowbird
25, 27

Tawny owl
40, 42

African forest elephant
58

Keel-billed motmot
53, 54

Toco toucan
64, 67

African leopard
51

Lesser rhea
61, 62

Wattled crane
49, 51

Andean night monkey
29, 31

Magellanic penguin
60-61, 62

White-breasted sea eagle
34

Annamite striped rabbit
37, 39

Marvellous spatuletail
29, 30

White egret
66

Asian elephant
81, 83

Military macaw
18

White-eared puffbird
84-85, 87

Azara's night monkey
85, 87

Neblina metaltail
31

White-necked parakeet
72-73, 75

Baird's tapir
46

Northern screamer
68, 70

Wreathed hornbill
12-13, 15

Bengal tiger
81, 83

Ocellated turkey
44, 46

Yellow-shouldered parrot
8-9, 10

Bezoar goat
21, 22

Oriental dwarf kingfisher
12, 15

Yellow-headed parrot
44-45, 47

Black bear
19

Red-chested owlet
26

Black rhino
24, 27

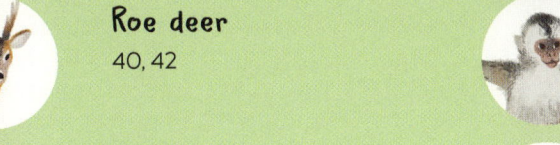

Marine mammals

Acknowledgements

DK would like to thank Dan Bradbury, Emma Douglas, José Rojo Martin, and the rest of the team at World Land Trust for their guidance, patience, and knowledge about all things wild.

Picture Credits

The publisher would like to thank the following for their kind permission to reproduce their photographs:(Key: a-above; b-below/bottom; c-centre; f-far; l-left; r-right; t-top)

6 Getty Images: Eamonn M. McCormack (tr). 7 World Land Trust: Roberto Pedraza, GESG (br). 10 Alamy Stock Photo: Urs Fleler (tc); Olga Sapegina (c); Konrad Wothe (bc). Getty Images / iStock: twildlife (crb). 11 Alamy Stock Photo: Arco / TUNS (bl); Brian Jannsen (cl); Janet Horton (cb). Shutterstock.com: Somyot Mali-ngam (bc). World Land Trust: Asociacin Civil Provita (tc). 14 123RF.com: Narupon Nimpaiboon (bc). Alamy Stock Photo: Agefotostock / Juan Carlos Muoz (tc). Dreamstime.com: Petr Maek / Petrmasek (cb). World Land Trust: HUTAN (cr). 15 Alamy Stock Photo: blickwinkel / F. Teiglar (bc); Zoonar GmbH / Nikolai Sorokin (bl). World Land Trust: David Bebber (tc); Kjersti Joergensen / Shutterstock.com (cl). 18 Alamy Stock Photo: John Cancalosi (tc); Mark Conlin (cra); David Havel (cb). naturepl.com: Claudio Contreras (bc). 19 Alamy Stock Photo: Dennis Binda (cb); David Chapman (cla); Horst Lieber (bl). naturepl.com: Roland Seitre (bc). World Land Trust: Roberto Pedraza, GESG (tc). 22 Alamy Stock Photo: funkyfood London - Paul Williams (bc). Getty Images / iStock: E+ / agustavop (tc). Getty Images / iStock: Londolozi Images / Mint Images (crb). World Land Trust: Gor Hovhannisyan / FPWC (c). 23 Getty Images: Raimund Linke (cla). World Land Trust: David Bebber (tc); William Gray (cb); Gareth Goldthorpe (bl). 26 Alamy Stock Photo: Krys Bailey (bc). Dreamstime.com: Volodymyr Byrdyak (tc). Getty Images / iStock: GomezDavid (cb). 27 Dreamstime.com: Nico Smit / Ecophoto (cla); Spaceheater (bc). World Land Trust: A. Buonajut (cb); Nature Kenya (tc); FLPA / Neil Bowman (bl). 30 Alamy Stock Photo: John Warburton-Lee Photography / Nigel Pavitt (tc); Micha Klootwijk (cra); Francesco Puntiroli (bc). 31 Alamy Stock Photo: Ryan M. Bolton (bc); Nature Picture Library / Kevin Schafer (cb); imageBROKER / Thomas Vinke (bl). World Land Trust: NCP (tc); Steve Snchez (cla). 34 Alamy Stock Photo: Toby Gibson (tc); Dray van Beeck (bc). Dreamstime.com: Donyanedomam (cra); Shane Myers (bc). 35 Alamy Stock Photo: WaterFrame_tat (bl). Dorling Kindersley: David Peart (clb); Linda Pitkin (bc). Getty Images / iStock: davidevison (cl). World Land Trust: Toby Gibson (tc). 38 123RF.com: Chaovarut Sthoop / kungverylucky (crb). Alamy Stock Photo: Ch'ien Lee / Minden Pictures (bc); Alison Teale (tc). Getty Images / iStock: 2630ben (c). 39 Alamy Stock Photo: naturephotos8 (cla). Dreamstime.com: Edwin Butter (c); Galinasavina (bl). Shutterstock.com: Galina Savina (bc). World Land Trust: David Bebber (tc). 42 Dreamstime.com: Urospoteko (c). World Land Trust: Gwynne Braidwood (bc); Mary Tibbett (tc); Sylvia Fresson / www.seeing.org.uk (cr). 43 Alamy Stock Photo: Martin Hughes-Jones (bl); Tierfotoagentur / K. Luehrs (cb). Dorling Kindersley: Sean Hunter Photography (cl). Dreamstime.com: Thomas Langlands (bc). World Land Trust: Audrey Welsh (tc). 46 Alamy Stock Photo: Arco / G. Lacz (cr); Alfredo Matus (tc); Kerry Hargrove (cb); Ray Wilson (bc). 47 Alamy Stock Photo: Claudio Contreras (bc); JPTenor (cl). World Land Trust: Enrique Aguirre / Shutterstock (cb); WLT / Christina Ballinger (tc); Erni / Shutterstock (bl). 50 123RF.com: Maurizio Giovanni Bersanelli (c). Alamy Stock Photo: Penny Boyd (bc); Nick Garbutt (tc). Dreamstime.com: Ecophoto (crb). 51 Alamy Stock Photo: Nigel Dennis (bc). Dreamstime.com: Lauren Pretorius (cb). naturepl.com: Bernard Castelein (cl). Shutterstock.

com: feathercollector (bl). World Land Trust: David Bebber (tc). 54 Dreamstime.com: Pedro Campos (cb); Softlightaa (tc). naturepl.com: Barry Mansell (cr). World Land Trust: Carlos Vsquez Almazn (bc). 55 Alamy Stock Photo: FLPA (cb). Dreamstime.com: Linnette Engler (cla). inaturalist.org: Wouter Beukema (bc). World Land Trust: FUNDAECO Archive (tc). 58 Alamy Stock Photo: Steve Bloom (cb); Roger de La Harpe / Biosphoto (cra); Clement Philippe (bc). Shutterstock.com: Anastasia Leonidova (tc). 59 Alamy Stock Photo: Max Allen (bl); eddylush (cl). Dreamstime.com: Happyshoot (c). Getty Images: Cagan Hakki Sekercioglu / Moment (bc). World Land Trust: Deng Deng National Park (tc). 62 Alamy Stock Photo: Chris Stenger / Buiten-Beeld (c); Michele Falzone (tc); James Caldwell (crb). Dreamstime.com: Davemhuntphotography (bc). 63 Alamy Stock Photo: J M Barres / agefotostock (bc); WaterFrame_fba (cl); David Tipling Photo Library (bl). World Land Trust: Leandro Legarreta / FPN (tc); Scott Guiver (clb). 66 Alamy Stock Photo: Helissa Grndemann (tc); Octavio Campos Salles (bc); Daniel Zupanc (cra). 67 Dorling Kindersley: Thomas Marent (bc). World Land Trust: Pepe Cartes (cb); Alan Martin (tc); Lee Dingain (bl). 70 123RF.com: Jiri Hrebicek (cb). Alamy Stock Photo: Pete Oxford / Minden Pictures (cra); Jess Kraft / Panther Media GmbH (tc). World Land Trust: Mauricio Rivera Correa (bc). 71 Alamy Stock Photo: Azoor Wildlife Photo (cb); Nature Picture Library (cla). Shutterstock.com: Guillermo Ossa (bc). World Land Trust: ProAves (tc, bl). 74 Alamy Stock Photo: David Tipling Photo Library (cr); Pete Oxford / Minden Pictures (c). Shutterstock.com: Ecuadorpostales (tc). World Land Trust: Sarah Barton (bc). 75 Alamy Stock Photo: Ignacio Yufera / Biosphoto (cla); Glenn Bartley / All Canada Photos (bc). Dreamstime.com: Brian Magnier (cb). naturepl.com: Agustin Esmoris (bl). World Land Trust: Nigel Simpson (tc). 78 Alamy Stock Photo: Amazon-Images (c); Michael Evershed (cr); Glenn Bartley / All Canada Photos (bc). World Land Trust: Asociacin Armona / Bennett Hennessey (tc). 79 Alamy Stock Photo: Glenn Bartley / All Canada Photos (clb); Alexandre Rotenberg (cla); Anton Sorokin (bc). Dorling Kindersley: Andy and Gill Swash (bl). World Land Trust: Sebastian Herzog (tc). 82 Alamy Stock Photo: Sylvain Cordier / Biosphoto (cr); Scenic landscape of Kodaikanal hill-station (tc). Dreamstime.com: Hedrus (ca). Getty Images / iStock: Casper1774Studio (bc). 83 Alamy Stock Photo: Arindam Bhattacharya (c); Ryhor Bruyeu (bl); frames (bc). World Land Trust: Christopher Kray (cla); WTI (tc). 86 Alamy Stock Photo: Krys Bailey (bc); Florian Kopp / imageBROKER (tc); Thomas Vinke / imageBROKER (cra); Kevin Schafer / Minden Pictures (cb). 87 Alamy Stock Photo: Sean Crane / Minden Pictures (cla); Pardofelis Photography (bc); Leonardo Mercon / VWPics (cb). Dorling Kindersley: Andy and Gill Swash (bl). World Land Trust: Tatiana Galluppi / Guyra Paraguay (tc). 95 World Land Trust: (tr); Nina Seale / WLT (tl); Tatiana Galluppi / Guyra Paraguay (tc, bc); HUTAN (tl); FUNDAECO Archive (c); David Bebber (cr); Tjalle Boorsma (clb); Lou Jost (crb)

All other images © Dorling Kindersley

Artwork © RIley Samels, 2022

Ranger Miguel, Mexico

Ranger Lourdes, Paraguay

Ranger Gwynne, United Kingdom

Ranger Eddie, Malaysian Borneo

Ranger Ricardo, Guatemala

Ranger Manuk, Armenia

Ranger Carlos, Bolivia

Ranger Carolina, Paraguay

Ranger Santiago, Ecuador

DK | Penguin Random House

Editor Vicky Armstrong
Project Art Editor Jon Hall
Designer Maisy Ruffels
Picture Researchers Martin Copeland,
Taiyaba Khatoon, and Aditya Katyal
Production Editor Siu Yin Chan
Senior Production Controller Louise Minihane
Senior Acquisitions Editor Katy Flint
Managing Art Editor Vicky Short
Publishing Director Mark Searle

Written by Lily Dyu
Illustrated by Riley Samels

First published in Great Britain in 2022 by
Dorling Kindersley Limited
DK, One Embassy Gardens, 8 Viaduct Gardens, London SW11 7BW

The authorised representative in the EEA is
Dorling Kindersley Verlag GmbH, Arnulfstr. 124, 80636 Munich, Germany

Page design copyright © 2022 Dorling Kindersley Limited
A Penguin Random House Company
10 9 8 7 6 5 4 3 2 1
001–328614–Jul/22

WORLD
LAND
TRUST

A CIP catalogue record for this book is available from the British Library.
ISBN 978-0-2415-5751-8

Printed and bound in Slovakia

For the curious

www.dk.com

FSC
www.fsc.org
MIX
Paper from
responsible sources
FSC™ C018179

This book is made from
Forest Stewardship Council™
certified paper—one small
step in DK's commitment
to a sustainable future.